THE ABANDONED SETTLEMENT

THE ABANDONED SETTLEMENTS

James Sheard

CAPE POETRY

Published by Jonathan Cape 2017

2 4 6 8 10 9 7 5 3 1

First published in Great Britain in 2017 by
Jonathan Cape
20 Vauxhall Bridge Road,
London SW1V 2SA

www.vintage-books.co.uk

A Penguin Random House Company

global.penguinrandomhouse.com

A CIP catalogue record for this book is available from the British Library

ISBN 9781910702475

Penguin Random House is committed to a sustainable future for
our business, our readers and our planet. This book is made from
Forest Stewardship Council® certified paper

Typeset in India by Thomson Digital Pvt Ltd, Noida, Delhi

Printed and bound in Great Britain by TJ International Ltd, Padstow, Cornwall

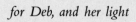

for Deb, and her light

CONTENTS

THE ABANDONED SETTLEMENTS

LINE BREAK

We're all pilgrims. We're all
more or less aware of that.

THE ABANDONED SETTLEMENTS

Think of it like this. The spine you once caressed
is the bony turf at Wharram, the only thing left
of the walls that held you, the hearth that warmed you.

And there are still lights, they say, in a back room
in Miaoulis Street, Varosha — somewhere inside, beyond
the bleached door frame and hinge splintered by decades of wind.

It's like that. It's like the sands where once you might have watched
a lover coming wet and lovely towards you — undisturbed now
and colonised by the shyest of creatures. It's the lone tower

at Wilmarsdonk — its bell gone and the church it served
now flattened, its weeded roof level with the crane tops
and high above the hollow bangs of containers setting down.

It's the wiped-out and the martyred. It's the places struck
from all your maps — the signs torn down, and the roads
to nowhere blocked for good measure. It's Oradour

and Wittenoom, and all the rust and rubble fall, the hulks
and helplessness, the townscapes like a dead flat tyre.
Think of how it twitches in our backbone, is seen dimly

through the window at night, how it walks towards us
in a stranger's body. How it sets itself in high memorial
above the utter transformation of our lives. Love, that is:

For love exists, and then is ruined, and then persists.

CARDAMOM

Me, I'm in a place
that once mattered,
but no longer matters –
and I figure, since it's late,
that you're hungering
for something that is like bread
but is not bread. That outside,
there's the open weave of the wind;
that there's the night
and its usual practices.

And I imagine
that you've been reading,
but it's the sort of reading
that feels like inhaling rain;
so you step out, and your shadow
is lying long on the lawn;
the flint of you is sparking,
and bits of you are flying upwards,
lodging in the night's lung.

Yes, I'm in one of those places
that once mattered,
but no longer matter – perhaps
the alley bar, at our back table,
its scratches since sanded off
and its surface newly varnished;
or the dry bowl of earth
beneath a weeping willow,
where we waited for the cold
and marvelled when it came.

And we know, you and I,
that there are some losses
which are nothing more
than a train slipping on an incline
in icy weather;
and that there are those
which derail everything,
blowing a hole in the house wall,
and leaving the wind to howl
around an empty chair. So

I'm in a place that once mattered,
but no longer matters,
and am not granted the space and time
to sing you back. But
I wondered if you, too,
are biting down on me now –
biting down, as if
on a split and softened
pod of cardamom –
on that bitter perfume,
on that medicinal heat.

ON READING

When I read it – the past –
I do not check my facts.
I only know that a man
whose name I cannot recall
reads from a forbidden text,
one which he has memorised.

He reads aloud, and I think I hear
the clamour of those who are tasked
to end him and the text he reads.
They get closer. But on he speaks,
and feels as though alone
on a patch of sand –

a beach, perhaps, or no, a place
dislocated from any landscape.
He is lonely – although there are listeners,
listeners who have grown ghostly,
as the man himself stiffens
into immobility.

And in the end,
there are only the words,
curling around him
like a whirlwind – the words
and the whipped-up sand.

And perhaps that is how reading
should always be.

And when I read it again, the past,
it is something else. Now
I am the man, standing
by a bookcase in a shop
and the book I hold is one
I cannot remember. It holds a poem
I think I know. I am tired.
My nerves are frayed.

There is music, but its strangeness
makes it of a kind
that I cannot place – atonal
and juddering alongside the line
I read and read again
and cannot quite decipher.

And I too am on a patch of sand,
aware of my text with a clarity,
and in a fog, and knowing
with a dim and final sense
that the approaching noise
will overwhelm and end me.

III

Right now, I am reading it –
the past. I am in a place

which overlooks fields and a river.
I have learnt that each night

the river dreams itself a body.
It rises long and laid-out

to the top of the treeline,
as if pinned, or held on stilts.

And it – whether the body, the reading or the past –
does not last the morning. It lasts

no longer than it takes the unharried sheep
to move like oxen, from one field to another.

WHITE ROSES

Well, I know what it's like:
you have been walking your room,

sniffing at your white roses
and shivering. There is a sip

of almond liquor in a glass
on your desk, and a note.

You are aware of your heartbeat,
and your hands shake, so that

your cigarette arrives clumsily
at your lips. How you hate it –

the black, glistening night,
the programmatic *blah-blah*

of love and its attendants.
Oh, you have been reading

The Sense of an Ending.
You have made some notes.

BLACKTHORN

For two weeks I drove
through tunnels
of March blackthorn,
leaving you lying
behind me and liquid
growing white
then full then falling
in the wind rising
each overnight
and becoming bridal
blizzarding across
the quiet early morning
whipped up by my wheels
leaving the iron thorns
of their hoops to grip
the root of me and hold me.

FALLING

He was the sort of boy who thought the world was his
to eat. You could see how a girl might fall for that.

He would scour away the trivial stuff with the acids
of his mouth – the various forms of flesh, the vegetation,

the soil and its underskin of rock – roll them into morsels
with his tongue and wash them down with great draughts of sea.

He would crack the mantel with those strong crooked teeth
and let the hot stuff gush into the declivities and sockets of his head.

You could see how a girl might fall for that, watching
the tense movement at his jawline, the glowing eyes.

And with the plates cracked, and the molten light shrivelling
the lesser men, he would spit out clinker and fire. You could see

how a girl might fall for that. And when he got there,
to the dense ball at the core, to the place where the metals had sunk

and gobstoppered themselves into a smoky-shiny marble –
well, it was a weight to sit in his gut, and his alone, held

by the bands of muscle beneath his faded shirt.
You could see how a girl might fall for that.

NOVEMBER

Let me tell you how, in this long dark,
I list the ways in which the leaf of you
unfurled and furled around me.

It is a thought like woodsmoke
entering the blood – the chambers
of the heart can only clutch at it.

THE GHOST IN YOUR
BURNING BUILDING

I watch you pause in your dressing,
fold an arm across a bare shoulder
and sit down on a bed that is rarely made.

The telly tracks up the floors
of the burnt-out house. The fireman
has never seen such a burning –

the shell gutted, the neighbours untouched.
But I have, I hear you mutter, skin
prickling. *Once, and years ago.*

I know that beneath your bed
are the coils of dust
and the oxblood suitcase.

Inside the case is the book
and the number to call –
there is a phone by the window,

and beyond the window,
the street and the workbound morning
and the waiting man.

So trap the receiver with a bony chin
and open the book –

Because I am not the man
who did the burning.

I am just the man
who knows your story.

I know the way that you would sit,
like that, half-naked upon your bed.

I know your skin.
I know your habits,

and how your voice would sound
on a cradled phone.

And I desire you, yes,
and so I place you there,
at a moment of distress,
between the past I know
and the present I imagine.

But I was not the man
who did the burning.

You sat in the car, the seat hot,
and could not make your eyes move away
from the hem of your short skirt.

You were defiant. No one would lay their hands
upon you, as the Romans did their slaves.
Emancipation, you said. *That's what it means.*

That evening, your friends were kind. For a while
there was a sense of female conspiracy – and yet
there was a lot of me still buried beneath that rubbish.

Later, you told me that you were mostly thinking
of the way you had of leaning back
and smiling knowingly. You knew

all about the provocative tilt
of your head. You knew you were
the *advocatus diaboli*, and that I

had soft and curious lips.

KNEELING

Really,
the only word
is the word
spoken into
your body
when I kneel
to you, all
foolish and
penitent.

ROOM

I've got, you wrote, *the blues.* It struck me
how the marginal anachronism of the phrase

marked the gap in our ages. I knew
that you quite enjoyed the feeling:

staying in bed, pulling the quilt up
to your throat, the warmth rising

to the tips of my hair. I pictured
your walls. A blown-up facsimile

of a letter Rosa Luxemburg wrote
to a friend from prison; a Japanese

paper butterfly, set at an angle;
a poster from *Les Enfants du Paradis.*

Will we fall into sterile bits and pieces,
you asked, or be put apart and together again,

Like stones in a child's game?
I do not know, but will not laugh,

not be flattered when you tell me
of my strange kind of dignity.

LETTERS, LIGHT

In here is the light
falling on a bed
and on a book left open
at a chapter you might read
a light you could put
your fingers into
testing it like a wound
to see how much
you could bear

there's the light
still low still crisp
in the park near *Erpel*
where the single blokes
and old limping men
would walk the paths
and look a light too hot
so you would go home
lie on your bed cool down
and touch yourself

there is the light here
the spring sun pouring
through orange curtains
and dimmed a little
by their double cloth
where you lie and relax
in this heap of pages
in its twilight and think
of how out of the world
one feels when one opens
the sluices.

PLUMB-LINE

The time will come
when fingers moving
restless on a table-top
will touch a thread
and find its loop
and drop a plumb-line
clean down through me.

I'll feel it fall. I'll feel it
fall until its weight
strikes stone and rests
in the haunted place
at the core of me.

SIGNALS

It was dark outside and the evening had fallen
unnoticed. I wanted to leave some sound

a signal, weak or strong – because you needed
to take weakness as seriously as strength.

We seemed to fear that talking might violate
our fertile isolations. Well, dear, there was solidarity there,

and hate – the fear of being sucked out and of sucking.

And so we lived in the time-lapse of letters,
moving like the rhythm of the slowest lovemaking.

And now I wish I had one from you to drink from.

THE HOLY WEDDING

Think of it, the Holy Wedding –
the young man in Spring,
sacrificed in Autumn.

Think of how women make
a God/Man to live out
their dreamlife for them.

Me, I would dream myself
into something, pull you out
into the light, you battering away

at my chest. I would pull you
down onto wet rainy grass,
your face still surprised

and smiling in disbelief.

LONG

I long to laze again on the dirty sand
beside the Elbe and not to know
what the business of *longing* is about
long to have that green coat again
to wrap it around you long to hear
you mumble *sorry we have stumbled
over each other* long for the bodies
which lie around as if waiting long
to watch you bite the top of your pen
and think yourself wise long to hear you
read out an essay on the dangers
of becoming inhuman or human

I forget which

on the long beach longing to bury
my head in your hollows longing
to hear again the scorn of that quip
*you think of ashes before you think
to light the fire*

LANDINGS

We wanted a land where we could watch the weather –
see how one hill drew down the drapes of rain, and how another
would flash its skin in a fall of sunlight.

We wanted a land where the roads barreled straight
over high, dry plains, the soil cooled to the frost-point.
It would stir in our drag, but show no sign of our passing.

At night, we said, we would drink peach nectar,
and we would seem to taste it all the way down,
from its fur right into its ragged stone – and then, asleep,

one of us would dream a line so sad and sweet
it would fuck us up forever – as if we could be so again,
and as if such words had ever pulled clear

from the fog of waking and forgetting. Yes,
we wanted a land where we might fall together,
then fail to wake – or, at least, to sleep beyond

the nag of morning, dragging us to its terraces
and its coffee and tobacco, taken slow and strong;
to where every distant view was wrong.

SCENT

The past is there
like a scent, armfuls
of it, arches of it,
lifted, steadied hips
of it, all the rolling
lilting movement of all
of it, fresh clay
of the skin and
the smell of home
in the hair. It is
a casket, split open
and then
closed to me
again.

RIVAL

We all have them –
the ones who lie beyond
the wall of operators
and dead numbers, beyond
the weeping woman
and the one who demands
to know your business.
We all can call
the might-as-well-be-dead.

One night, she dialled,
made notes, re-dialled.
She was thinking of him,
the man-in-the-sun,
marching beside her
with those upper arms
she always wanted to bite,
full-jawed, as if breaking
an apple open.

And she saw his fingers,
blunt-ended, twisting fast
around the incendiary's wires.
He was the man that she would fuck
from time to time – once,
and never again,
then again.

So on she dialled, years
beyond me. Until she heard
his rattling voice, and I
watched her bear down
upon that simmer of pleasure.

NOTE FOR YOU

Yes, there's another woman
on the next page –
you won't like her at all.

I face you both.
I face them all.
I justify myself
like a convict.

So back me up. Just
back me up.

THE SUIT

She had kept it for years, the suit.
Ready for his return, ready
for the time he would clatter again
through that door that broke knuckles
if not handled right. He would ask for it:
Where's the suit? Show me the suit!

It had hung there, the suit. Hung
from its line of wire and dust, hung
in the closed-off block of air
that smelt of suit, and of all the things
they'd wanted.

He'd try it on, *she thought*, and she
would help him – fussing a little
at the set of his shoulders, the tightness
at the waist. I will nip my tongue
between my teeth, *she thought*, and furrow
my brow, like so. I will be lovely, utterly lovely,

as a woman like me should be when bent
to such small and loving tasks.

CAZZO DI RE

Towards sunset, we walked out
onto a ledge of cracked rock and fished.
You lent me the rod you had used as a boy,
and took your father's.
This pleased you.

We picked small shellfish
from among the accretions of fossils.
We crushed them for bait,
then cast out for the King's Shit,
moving silver and blood-streaked
in the evening water. I only liked
my occasional throw of the line,
and the waiting. I caught nothing.
I was happy.

The next morning, your father
drove us to a place of sullen barter,
lifted a half-case of wine from his boot,
swapped it for a net bag of clams
and a pair of sea bass.
He gutted the fish at the harbour wall,
flicking the intestines out to the gulls,
and glowering at us.

Later, up there, on the long rock
of houses and narrow streets,
your family mainly silent and watchful
with the stranger, we ate it all –
the clams gritty and sweet in pasta,
the bass *not messed-about-with*. I thought
of how often I had said *vill-idge,*
not *vill-ahge,* and how you always forgot.

But tell me, Giusepp', why I was there.
It was scarcely a holiday. We were barely friends.
Was it perhaps about how it felt
to live in the tight orbit of those men –
the tense little tyranny of the father,
the crippled *Nono* under the terrace myrtle,
the uncles baying for homage in the bars?

When it was all back to normal,
we would meet in the streets
of our Northern town – you hunched
against the rain in a stockman's coat,
slurred and slow from late shifts,
bewildered by the demands of English women
and their solemn, sad critiques. You would cast
into me, again and again, and hook nothing.
I had no time, and no advice for you,
beyond to say *I agree. It would have killed you,*
just a little faster than this will.

I am on the ferry, crossing
the second gap.

There's a woman
in my cabin. I think she, too,

could be a daughter –
very slim and very bitter.

SHADOW SELF

for Joe Stretch

He walks here still,
your shadow self.
He's got your back
and the boots you left.
He's got your gait,
but stole your health.
He walks here still,
your shadow self.

He's living it,
your shadow life.
He owns your flat
and fucks your wife.
He lives it loose,
but holds it tight.
He's loving it,
your shadow life.

Hamburg 2012

SHE READS MY STORY

This is how you see yourself, *she tells me* –

The rain biblical, the little boy lost,
the market street as broad as a river.
The gutters can't cope and it's Sunday,
Sunday, and shut, and shelter is nowhere –
and you walk, because to run is unlike you.
And the place you find has a window
with a drawn blind, and a light behind,
and a door, and a sign in small letters.

And when you make me, *she says* –
you make me flat and focused
like something drawn out
from a single pearl of ink.
You make this thing stand against the light.
You make it talk like me.
You set an unseen clock ticking
and scuff my floor with leaves and mud.

And on she went, feeling her way
to the borders of my story –
to the bloom of her anger,
to the stopping of the clock,
and to the far door opening
onto the workshop of memory
which lay beyond.

PASS

Later, I rubbed honey on your gums
to bring you round. It was

like that, sometimes. And for all
we'd gasp and laugh at what we'd done,

we really knew that through our peaks
ran a coldness like a pass.

LEAVING

I spoke a lot
about leaving that day,
and each time
the word left me,
it tolled
like a leavers' bell.

That night, each time
your face came to me,
I waved it away.
I was longing for sleep.

And then my sleep
was a lake,
and you were the land –
you held me,
all the way round,
and yet still it felt
as though I had lost you.

We stepped off the small plane into landing strip spindrift,
glittering like coils of electric dust around our boots. *Real flying, that*
the man behind me said – *you could feel it all.*

The air plucked out the heart. We adjusted our breathing
and filed to the waiting truck, its fat nose trembling. SISU,
it said, SISU. So we endured its metal cave, our eyes on our toecaps.

It took us to a clearing, and to sips of something hot –
cloudberry vapour rising, feet stamping, as we watched
the final freeze being layered on a house built of ice.

We tramped through the flat acoustics of its corridors,
climbed its rough-sawn stairs, were told of the utter
dreamlessness of the sleep that could be had there.

But not for us. For we still dreamt, and were waiting
for the brief, uncertain dark, for the time when we might at last
walk out into our territory. When it came, we each would carry

the pocketed embers of our various loves. Each would bear
a still-glowing torch. We would pass through a darkness
of glassy, splitting trees to the lake. And there,

we would scatter what was left on its stony white slab
and watch them blacken. We would thrust our hot brands hard
through the crust of the snows, and extinguish them,

and then lay ourselves down and watch the last rising
of our warmth, our breath thinning as the cold took us.
And in its merging, it would remake that lying moon of yours.

CINEMA

Lately,
I seem to have lost
my art of sitting,
of knowing
how each limb
should lie,
or tell some truth.

DEDICATION

You are scattered about the stone temples —
made of poor-fired clay, or carved
from soft rock — figurines of you,
seen from down there, down between
the spread thighs which loom and fill
the vision, the cunt crude and flared,
the upper body foreshortened.
Because their carvers too had been there,
held, adoring, and looking up. They too
had walked the mazes and the temples,
the chambers shaped like that — the tight entrance,
the paths which looped into mystery,
the whole formed like a dipped bull's head
with curved-in horns. Thinking of it,

and with you before me, I wonder
at how even the cloth which has touched it
is precious to me — like a relic dipped
in the wound of a saint. And then it comes —
the sweet sinking feeling, my proud ship
holed, the wide gash in its side. I go down
beneath the slow swell of your waterline.
I ache for it, ache for it, and so will take
the wet and the flow of you, the sweet
and the sharp, the clear and the pearly,
the crimson, the dark — take it down in me
and over me and into me.

And I would learn for you a new way
of breathing — so that I might drown in you,
and yet be brought up, dripping and awake,
to be plunged down again. I would learn
to be buried in you, and come back

with the smeared burst fruits of you
stopping my mouth and throat, making me
sweeter and refreshed. So take me
by my horns. Bow my big head to you
to that melting and that burial.

I have often told myself to keep them strong,
the wingbeats of my telling. Make them move

the air above the lost places, lift the dust from
the abandoned counters, make the door swing

and the broken window drop another dagger
of glass. But today,

the wind moaned in the gutter like a calling-out.
I could only hold my body neat, and neglected.

My mouth worked as if unwillingly. The bell
in some close tower tolled and the the birds rose

and carried each word away, speaking it to any ear
that would listen.

DUTIES

He had been out there as usual,
on the backstep by the bins
when his heart did that thing again –
its chamber failing to fill, then flipping over
like a muscly fish, all fat and wet
then thumping once and hard,
and going on. *Everyone gets that*
the Doctor had said, *at least every now and then.*

Upstairs, the door to his mother's room
is slightly open. His brother's abroad.
She's still not speaking, mourning one
and punishing the other. He wonders
what that light is – too faint to be a lamp –
that makes the glazed door glow.

He puts the kettle on the stove, spoons honey
into a tall glass. The kettle breathes and rattles.

When anxious or bitter about her sons,
she tells him of a visitation. Thickening
from the darkness of her room, an old woman
forms herself and approaches the bed.
She wears a bonnet like the old ones wore.
She says nothing, his mother tells him
but looks so untroubled. My worry fades.
He, too, can be the bringer of peace.

He sets down the glass beside her.
The way she shapes herself beneath the cover
is a symbol for him to read.

He rinses the glass in the small kitchen
and sets the spoon down on the drainer
with a click. The buildings opposite are darker now
because the sky has lightened.
He, too, can be the bringer of peace.

THE CRADLE

And I'll tell you all over, if allowed
of how I always loved you. That yes,
it was a love I often cradled much too close.

But I would ask you to let yourself think
of what such a cradling is like –
of the children we each have held,
close, and lifted into ourselves. To think

of how our backs must sometimes turn,
our shoulders hunch, to shield the love
from all that the world has dealt us.

So whatever you believe of me,
and whatever I must now live with,
do not believe that in that cradling
I would have sought to stifle what I held.

SCULPTRESS

The sculptress was unblessed, felt
no light on her forehead.

She had made five female statues
and a phallus.

I would have the latter cast in bronze
if I ever had the money.

She walked the earth
in a cloud of plaster and dust,

clay under her nails.

LIBRARY

I cannot recall how many times
I made you drop me off there.
The car would cool, and, for a while
it seemed that I wore your shadow
like a hat brim — before pulling myself clear
and shutting you off
with the gentlest of clicks.

I clattered up the steps
of the marbled hallway,
like a handful of stones
carried in a pocket.
Inside, I fouled the mirrors,
scuffed the skirting and the veneer
of the attendant's empty desk.

When I think of it now, it is as though
I open one eye onto darkness.
I sense you moving
like knuckles across a fat hand.
And out there, I think,
a night librarian is restless.
She runs a finger along my spine,
my shelving.

There is something to place
before the ones we profess to love –
a bowl of something, bright things,
the brimming of gems of fruit,
or just-broken buds, something fresh
and wet in the breakfast light.

There is something to offer. Something
to cup in our curved palms, a bowl
of something warm, its curled sides
fragrant with rising vapours,
or the cooler scents of long caring.
Something for them to dip their heads to,

or to lift their heads from, nourished,
to see how the sky still shivers like a bell.

His name means *close-fitting, tight, just-there*,
his plates of armour inched together
and held to seal in something of a past and a pain.

And we are all artists of ourselves. We all do it –
apply material to our naked surfaces,
paint ourselves thickly for the world,
or scrape ourselves back to our rawness.

When we choose our colours,
some reduce themselves to the strictest palette,
and some clutter it all up, until no one knows
quite what lies beneath.

Creams. Greens. The torn-off section of an insect.
Look away, *it says*, let your eye be repelled,
or skitter across my metal in an arc. Let your eye
move to the eye that watches you back.
Be deflected to my edges, and away.

Later, Stefan will snap his plates
still closer together, flatten and brighten
the colours, cover every inch
with symbols and signs. Yes,

it all pushes us a little further off.
But think of a man driven to a mastery
of enamel on metal, driven to a perfection,
to the clicking-shut of closure – and all

because he once dropped and cracked
a young woman's pendant at a party,
and did not know how he might mend it.

TAN Y BWLCH

I have tried it before – to write the headland.
But there is the trickiness of coastlines –
distances which fool us, traced journeys seen
from a lifted land and its loftiness. This one

curtails the arc of the bay, calm-seeming
and waiting for the ships to be driven into it
and wrecked. The snouted cliff seems split
like a mouth. And lulled again, I think

of how we might round it, and move beyond.
Best not, for now. Best lie here beneath the loft-beams,
best make you cry out in the warm space
above the ghosts of livestock, gathered in

for the night – and as our beasts shift and stink
and are uncertain, their heat will rise
and rise to us.

FALLEN

sometimes you
step hesitantly
into my territory
at twilight
peering through
the dreamland
of tree bole
and bramble
of briarwork
and the broken walls
and there
on the churned earth
the bulk of a fallen beast
its side torn open
still steaming

I am there
I am curled up
wet and stained
held in its ropes
with the open skin
drawn back over me
lift me up
into the air
into the light of you
take me into your
arms and home
and clean me

FRENCH

We knew the way that dying
light made flags of colour.
We thought of it as French —
the purples and pinks striking out
in that late afternoon light.

The green foil of grass
and overlaid leaf-cover
blur and softened behind it,
disappearing early. But in front,

the colour as quick and loud
as artists brawling in a lit café —
their bright splashed canvases left

to dry in some spattered loft.

SWALLOW

Yes, keep yourself out of reach
of the lion's mouth.
Be among all the others,
but invisible.

Hope to form something
out of soft clay,
follow the lines with your hands
and slow eyes.

You were told to dance your pain,
but it was little,
with long arms and stretched-out fingers.
And again, you were told

to cut it into pieces and eat it,
and, defiant,
you tried to swallow it whole.
It was hard

to get its feet down – but harder still
was its head
bulging in your mouth, the sight
of its green-golden eyes.

LATE

You could be my garden, for think how gardens
can be our last and best love, our late love,
brought up and out of our earth and made to bloom.

Think how we bring to them our lifetime of care,
our longing for a place to lie in and call our own.
That is why I brought you here in late summer,

to watch you walk up through the blown grasses
and their feathery tops moving gently around you.
You came to me, slowly, down the long shade

of the laburnum arch, as if approaching shyly
from the long years of my early and middle life –
dappled and distant, but coming on, coming on.

BONE MUSIC

for Jacob Polley

This it is, then,
the bone music.
The one curls into the other
and breathes of how she once sat,
birdlike on the unmade bed, bent,
perhaps to hide her face,
or find her clothes.
I saw them then,
he says, *these flutes of bone,*
they still pipe clearly
through my head.

And here it is,
the bone duet, her singing
that she is still the bone,
the ringing bone, still blown
without breath – *still lifted,*
she says, *by the tilting*
of the clay, by the moving
of your fingers
at my jawline.

And if the earth spoke
about the bone music,
it might tell us how –
once their soft stuff
had leached into it,
and they stilled,
and it settled –
how it was then you could hear it.

Piped notes, it would say
moving through me
like worms.

So to get the measure
of the bone music,
mark out your ground
with lines, like a drawn stave.
And when they emerge
with the scrape of digging,
the feathery attentions of brushes,
it will be as though
two complex notes
sharpen into light.